BUBBLES, BANKERS & BAILOUTS

The GLOBAL FINANCIAL CRISIS *and* HOW YOU CAN SURVIVE IT

• • •

BUBBLES BANKERS & BAILOUTS

JOHN LAWRENCE REYNOLDS

Douglas & McIntyre

D&M PUBLISHERS INC.
VANCOUVER/TORONTO

09 10 11 12 13 5 4 3 2 1

Douglas & McIntyre
A division of D&M Publishers Inc.
2323 Quebec Street, Suite 201
Vancouver, BC Canada V5T 4S7
www.dmpibooks.com

Library and Archives Canada Cataloguing in Publication

Reynolds, John Lawrence
Bubbles, bankers & bailouts : the global financial crisis and
how you can survive it / John Lawrence Reynolds.

ISBN 978-1-55365-319-6

1. Finance, Personal—Canada. 2. Financial crises.
3. International finance. I. Title. II. Title: Bubbles, bankers and bailouts.

HB3722.R49 2009 332.02400971 C2009-900320-1

Editing by Barbara Czarnecki
Cover and text design by Ingrid Paulson
Cover photograph by © Tarhill Photos Inc./CORBIS
Printed and bound in Canada by Friesens
Printed on acid-free paper that is forest friendly (100% post-consumer
recycled paper) and has been processed chlorine free

We gratefully acknowledge the financial support of the
Canada Council for the Arts, the British Columbia Arts Council,
the Province of British Columbia through the Book Publishing Tax Credit
and the Government of Canada through the Book Publishing Industry
Development Program (BPIDP) for our publishing activities.

For Hans and Shannon Merkelbach

“Virtue does not come from money, but from virtue comes money and all other good things, both to the individual and to the state.”

SOCRATES

“There is enough money in the world for everyone’s need, but not for everyone’s greed.”

FRANK BUCHMAN

INTRODUCTION

How the economic crisis started . . . and how to ride it out

You tolerate your boss, pay your bills and taxes, feed and clothe the kids, make your mortgage payments, contribute to an RRSP, use your credit cards with prudence and manage to live in some contentment with your spouse.

And what happens? It's all threatened by people you never heard of in places you'll never visit spending amounts of money you'll only dream of on schemes you can't understand. Is this fair? No, it's reality.

Things were scary enough through the summer of '08 with Afghanistan, Iraq, al Qaeda, *C. difficile* and Sarah Palin to worry about. In September, news reports began warning of the risk of a recession shortly after Stephen Harper and George W. Bush declared that the economies of Canada and the United States were strong. Then two people you never heard of—Fannie Mae and Freddie Mac—announced they were broke. The U.S. federal government solved their problem by giving them hundreds of billions of dollars. How do you write a cheque for hundreds of billions of dollars? You don't. You crank up a printing press, let it run full speed over the weekend and ship the cash the next day.

Soon people whose names sound more familiar were also crying poor. They were Lehman Brothers and Bear Stearns. Meanwhile Merrill Lynch, the folks who were always bullish on America—now why would *they* need money?—sold themselves to the highest bidder. That's when stock markets around the world began to crumble.

You grew concerned. Brokers and financial advisers suggested you stay calm. "Stocks go up and stocks go down," they said. "Relax."

By October 2008 it was difficult to relax. The world's biggest insurance company, known as AIG, announced it was basically broke. How can an insurance company go broke? If too many claims arrive to be paid, an insurance company simply raises its premiums, doesn't it? What massive insurance claims sank AIG? Did another Hurricane Katrina, San Francisco earthquake or global tsunami drain the insurance company's piggy bank? One day AIG is sitting in an enormous skyscraper in Manhattan with limousines waiting to take its executives to lunch, and the next day it's in the Bowery, or wherever New York bums go, asking for spare change. Spare change in this case amounted to US$150 billion.

Through the rest of October the news grew worse. According to People Who Should Know, which includes TV news anchors, the *Wall Street Journal* and your brother-in-law who once owned shares in Bre-X, a recession loomed on the horizon or even around the corner. By November, stock prices were dropping faster than a naughty girl's knickers on New Year's Eve, and printing presses at the U.S. Mint kept churning out greenbacks. President George W. Bush promised to hand American businesses and banks an amount of money you could not envision or even believe. By mid-November the anticipated bailouts, including outright purchases of companies, looked like this:

TARP	$700 billion
Bear Stearns	$29 billion
GM, Ford and Chrysler	$25 billion
AIG	$150 billion
Fannie and Freddie	$200 billion
Mortgage-backed securities	$144 billion
FHA Rescue Bill	$300 billion
JPMorgan for Lehman Brothers	$87 billion

TAF program	$200 billion
Commercial paper	$50 billion
Fed currency swaps	$740 billion
TOTAL (*take a deep breath*):	$2.625 TRILLION

For those who really need to know what those terms mean:

TARP (TROUBLED ASSET RELIEF PROGRAM): Money for people who are supposed to know how to manage money but lost all of theirs, so American taxpayers will give them lots of their own cash.

MORTGAGE-BACKED SECURITIES: Pieces of paper representing thousands of mortgages on homes and office buildings.

FHA RESCUE BILL: Legislation passed by the U.S. Congress in the spring of 2008 authorizing the Federal Housing Authority to help American homeowners in danger of losing their homes because they couldn't meet their mortgage payments.

JPMORGAN FOR LEHMAN BROTHERS: Riding into Wall Street on a white horse, financier JPMorgan Chase & Co. bought its competitor Lehman Brothers to save it, using $87 billion from the U.S. Federal Reserve. Some reports claim another $51 billion was advanced the following day; others disagree. After the first $50 billion, who's counting?

TAF (TERM AUCTION FACILITY): A temporary (*sic*) program managed by the U.S. Federal Reserve designed to "address elevated pressures in short-term funding markets." Banks and other "depository institutions" that are "in generally sound financial condition" and "are expected to remain so over the terms of TAF loans" can borrow money for 28 or 84 days to tide them over until payday or next weekend's garage sale.

COMMERCIAL PAPER: Loans, extending from overnight to 270 days, that are made to large banks or companies that need cash to meet short-term obligations like a payroll or this month's payment on the corporate jet. They are backed only by a promise, which means if they can't pay it back they promise to have the government do it. Which is what happened to a lot of banks in the fall of 2008.

FED CURRENCY SWAPS: If a company in Canada wants to buy something from the United States, it must pay in U.S. dollars. To get them, it visits a bank and asks for $x million in Yankee greenbacks. If the bank doesn't have that much in Yankee dollars in its vault, it borrows it from another bank. But when things get tough, banks don't like making loans even to other banks. This makes it difficult to do business, so federal government bankers get on the telephone and call their counterparts in other countries saying something like, "If I send you $100 billion in greenbacks, will you send me $100 billion in loonies?" and "How about them Leafs?" The national banks make the foreign currency available to the private banks who need it.

With the exception of the imminent departure of George W. Bush from Washington, none of this was good news. The effect on Canada, however, would not be as disastrous as on the United States. Or so we were told.

By December people stopped mentioning recession and began dropping the D-word. A global depression appeared possible, if not imminent. The assets of General Motors, once the most valuable corporation in the world, were worth about as much as the average corner variety store.

The risk that the entire North American automotive industry could vanish became more real with every Chevrolet, Ford and Chrysler sitting unwanted on dealers' lots. While Toyota, Honda, Suzuki and other transplants might continue producing vehicles in North America, the loss of jobs at the Big Three automakers would strike a blow to the continent's economics that had never been witnessed before. The impact of several hundred thousand workers being unemployed in Canada would take years, even decades to correct.

Meanwhile the rest of the economy continued to slide and nobody appeared immune. If you were employed, you wondered how long you could keep your job. If you were retired, were about to retire or were still contributing to an RRSP, you watched the value of your investments dribble away like fine Merlot through a leaky bucket.

This was serious. Canadians began asking, Is the world economy truly collapsing around me? How could such a thing happen? Who caused it and how? And *what the hell can I do about it??!!*

The first thing you can do is stay calm and read this book.

Q: What the heck happened?

Money is like manure.
If you spread it around, it does a lot of good.
But if you pile it all up in one place,
it stinks like hell.

Clint Murchison, American industrialist

A: Want a scapegoat? Start with the United States. This is not unfair. For more than half a century, the United States has influenced global economics with far greater clout than any other country because its dollar is the principal reserve currency. A reserve currency is the money that countries hold in reserve to back their own currency, and it can be exchanged for any other currency. Instead of "reserve," think "universal" or "common denominator." That's been the role of the U.S. dollar in currency exchanges, and it's an important one. You can buy all the Mongolian tugriks or Paraguayan guaranis you need with U.S. dollars, but lots of luck buying a tugrik with a guarani. Both must be converted first into greenbacks and then into the desired currency, assuming anyone desires a pocketful of tugriks.

How can a small piece of paper command as much power in Kuala Lumpur as it does in Kansas? Until 1971 the answer was simple, and it was on every U.S. dollar bill. In theory, anyone with a Yankee dollar could exchange it for an equivalent amount of gold found in Fort Knox and other locations. Richard Nixon killed that idea, promising everyone that a dollar was still worth a dollar and his word was as good as gold, which may have started the whole mess right there. These days the American dollar, like the Canadian loonie and every other major currency, is backed not by gold but by a promise. And governments never break their promises, do they?

So the world's finances revolve around the U.S. dollar, and the U.S. dollar's ultimate home is no longer Fort Knox but Wall Street. Wall Street is notorious for creating new ways to make its inhabitants enormously wealthy, a pastime that became both easier and more profitable after 1980 thanks to deregulation. Ronald Reagan and both Bush presidents, believing the denizens of Wall Street were as innocent as Little Bo Peep's sheep, decided to leave them alone. Without regulators looking over their shoulders, the theory went, Lehman Brothers, Bear Stearns, Goldman Sachs, Merrill Lynch and dozens of other smaller, less prominent operations would be free to make everybody wealthier. And that's what happened, especially under the regime of the second George Bush.

From 2000 to 2007, members of the U.S. Congress banished laws that had prevented commercial banks, investment banks and insurance companies from forming private clubs. The new bills made it more difficult for consumers to get out from under punishing debts by declaring bankruptcy, and ordered federal watchdogs to stop policing banks, insurance companies, mortgage lenders and investment firms.

Unconstrained by both their elders and the general public, denizens of the financial and investment jungle began partnering with each other. Soon the entire financial and investment industry looked like a gang of sexual swingers at a Viagra convention, breeding and inbreeding up and down Wall Street and beyond. Their actions begat strange creatures no one had encountered before, identified by names such as credit default swaps, interest-rate derivatives, asset-backed commercial paper and other newly hatched offspring. Warren Buffett, who is both smarter and wealthier than any ten people you and I can name, called these beasts "financial weapons of mass destruction."

To put it in another context, the kids on Wall Street and their cronies all across the United States were given keys to the candy store. With nobody around to watch over them, they devoured toxic sweets such as sub-prime mortgages, which represented too much money invested in too many houses bought by too many people who couldn't afford to make the payments. The kids in the candy store got fat. Everyone else got arteriosclerosis.

EVERYBODY SHOULD OWN A HOME. BUT SHOULD EVERYONE HAVE A MORTGAGE?

Through the opening years of the twenty-first century, mortgage interest rates remained at historically low levels. Working-class families were able to purchase homes easily, new housing developments sprang up everywhere, and everyone prospered. Then greed took over.

For an entire decade, housing prices across North America resembled an ever-expanding bubble. Everyone believed a house purchased for $300,000 this year could be worth $330,000 next year and $350,000 the year after that, and for a few years they were proven correct. The gravy train was in town.

Mortgage brokers, encouraged by Clinton and Bush the Second, went to work assisting anyone who wanted to live the American Dream. Congress passed a bill in

1992 that required the mortgage guarantors Fannie Mae and Freddie Mac[1] to expand their portfolio and support lower-income (or "sub-prime") borrowers, defined as Americans whose annual income was 40 per cent or more below the national average. With the blessing of Fannie Mae and Freddie Mac and the active encouragement of Congress, banks and mortgage brokers began distributing money. Interest rates remained low and housing values continued climbing, making it easy for mortgage lenders to convince anybody earning as much as your average chimney sweeper to purchase a brand-new mini-castle. Residents of trailer parks with low credit ratings were told they could transform themselves into something they had never dreamed of becoming: homeowners (and mortgage owners as well, of course).

Banks and brokers began ignoring old-fashioned guidelines such as minimal down payment requirements. Who needs to put money down when the house will be worth 10 per cent more this time next year? To make things easier, interest on mortgages for the first

---

1 The full legal terms for these rather silly names are, respectively, Federal National Mortgage Association and Federal Home Loan Mortgage Corporation. Both were created as government-backed privately operated enterprises to package residential mortgages and sell them on the open market as investment opportunities. Similar operations with folksy monikers include Sallie Mae (Student Loan Marketing Association), Farmer Mac (Federal Agricultural Mortgage Corporation) and Ginnie Mae (Government National Mortgage Association).

year or two was calculated at a rate lower than the prime rate charged by banks when dealing with each other. This was essentially a teaser technique, attracting buyers with mortgage rates as low as 1 per cent annually for the first year or two. Later, when the house was worth more than the purchase price, the interest rate would be reset at a higher rate to make up the difference. And the difference was often considerable. Some proud new homeowners discovered their monthly payments of $800 or $900 had suddenly increased to $1,500 or more. As a result, the people who could least afford it found themselves paying the highest mortgage interest rate.

Banks had no problem accessing cash to cover these mortgages. Much of it was flowing back to the United States from China, whose currency was pegged at an artificially low level compared with the dollar, making its goods artificially low in price. Thanks to a growing flood of cheap products, China and other East Asian exporting countries were awash with greenbacks. China spent the cash on U.S. bonds, effectively loaning the money back to the people who were financing China's expansion.

This stream of cash back into the U.S. Treasury was critical because other sources were drying up. In normal times, banks earn profit from the difference between the interest they pay depositors who entrust them with their money, and the amount of interest the banks charge borrowers. With annual interest levels at a paltry 3 or 4 per cent, depositors began looking beyond their neighbourhood bank for higher earnings, an action financiers tag "a hunt for yield." When the hunters tracked down higher yields from investments based on sub-prime mortgages, they seized them.

In every investment you can name, from government bonds to lottery tickets, the only way to enjoy higher yield is to accept higher risk. Sub-prime mortgages were substantially more risky than conventional mortgages, but no one seemed to care.

As for the banks, in Wall Street terms they were borrowing short and lending long. They would tap a few billion in cash from the global money market over a six-month term and use it to cover a raft of twenty-five- or even forty-year mortgages granted to sub-prime customers. When the bank's six-month term required payback, they sold the mortgages to high-yield hunters, paid off the short-term loan, pocketed the profits, borrowed another billion or so over six months and launched yet another cycle.

In the jargon of the investment industry, the banks *securitized* their mortgages, meaning they wrapped them in pretty paper and sold them like fruitcakes at Christmas, severing the link between themselves and their mortgage clients. Consider the contrast between this approach and that of James Stewart in the iconic feel-good movie *It's a Wonderful Life.* Stewart's character, like his father before him, knew both the depositors who trusted the bank and the mortgage clients whom the bank trusted to pay their debt. The key word here is *trust.* With securitized mortgages, bundled with other debt from here and there, nobody knew whom to trust.

In 1994, when the idea was first hatched, sub-prime mortgages in the United States totalled a reasonable $35 billion. Barely ten years later they represented an unreasonable $625 billion—money owed to banks and financial institutions by people who, in many cases, would normally qualify for barely enough credit to purchase a floor lamp. Now they were homeowners. More critically, they were mortgage owners with payments, now or in the immediate future, that they had little hope of making past the artificially reduced schedule set for the first year or two.

GLOBALIZATION MEANS WE FEEL THEIR PAIN—EVERYWHERE

In the investment market, mortgages are bought and sold like stocks and bonds. Rolling sub-prime mortgages into multi-million-dollar packages along with a crazy-quilt mix of car loans, derivatives and other interest-paying assets, investment houses sold them on a wholesale level as asset-backed commercial paper, or ABCP, to brokers, dealers and other banks. These middlemen peddled them to pension funds and individual investors, most of whom slid the ABCP into their retirement savings portfolio. The ABCP investments were generally short-term vehicles—thirty- or sixty-day terms—that delivered relatively high interest payments at relatively low risk. And they were not restricted to the United States.

Globalization, and the expansion and merging of banks and investment houses, created a worldwide market for ABCP. It sounded and looked, on the surface at least, like an ideal investment vehicle, combining a higher yield than bonds and savings accounts with the security of residential mortgages. When the first wave of ABCP sold out, brokers and dealers demanded more, and lenders responded with new batches of securitized sub-prime mortgages packaged with a mixture of other investments such as collateralized debt obligations (CDOs) consisting of mortgages, loans, bonds and the odd kitchen sink—a mishmash whose risk could not be measured accurately. Soon investors were handing over cash for grab bags of securities that varied widely in quality, making it difficult to determine the true risk involved.

This did not stop professional ratings agencies around the world from blessing these mongrels. Investors rely on agencies, including Moody's, Standard & Poor's, A.M. Best Company and the Dominion Bond Rating Service (DBRS) in Canada, to assess the risk level of investments and classify them accordingly. The higher the rating the lower the risk, and the lower the risk the lower the returns paid to investors.

Stable governments and the bluest of blue-chip corporations earn an AAA rating from ratings agencies, indicating maximum security. From there, the ratings descend through AA and A to BBB ("acceptable assurance of a return of interest and principal"), BB, B ("a reasonably high level of uncertainty as to the ability of the entity to pay interest and principal on a continuing basis in the future"), CCC, CC, C ("retains features which, if not remedied, may lead to default") and D, whose DBRS rating can be loosely translated as "You've been had, sucker."

The problem with these services is that they derive their income not from investors, who are laying down money to purchase the investments, but from the people issuing or marketing the product. Can you see a conflict of interest here?

Countries like Canada, whose stuffy and conservative banks normally were as attracted to ABCP and sub-prime mortgages as the Queen is to cheap beer, absorbed a limited number of these securities. Still, a raft of them slipped across the border thanks to heavy lobbying by American firms such as GE Capital that demanded the same access to Canada as they enjoyed in their home territory.

More than half of the ABCP arriving in Canada found its way into Quebec's huge pension fund, the Caisse de dépôt et placement du Québec, while Alberta's provincially owned ATB Financial reportedly purchased about $1 billion in ABCP. Private investors who put their money and their trust in ABCP paid heavily. About fourteen hundred Canadians spent a total of $269 million to purchase ABCP from Vancouver-based Canaccord Capital Inc. Lawsuits have been threatened by investors, who claim they were never told the true risk of investing in these dogs, and by Canaccord, which claims that DBRS hung an undeserved R1 rating, its equivalent of AAA, on these risky packages.

Back in the United States, no red lights were flashing to warn of the dangers involved in ABCP. Everybody was seeing green, as in the colour of money. Lenders were making profits by issuing mortgages to almost anyone who walked through the door. Building contractors were setting records constructing new houses for people who had been living in cold-water flats most of their lives. Carpenters, bricklayers, electricians, painters, plumbers, furniture dealers all began working overtime. Waves of joy and prosperity swept across the land.

For the first three-quarters of the decade, we all believed we were part of an economic paradise, a world where almost everyone prospered with no end of the party in sight. In reality, we were involved in a giant Ponzi scheme that ultimately, inevitably had to come crashing down.[2]

The people who assembled these deals, wherein houses were sold to buyers who had little hope of covering their mortgage payments once realistic interest rates applied, walked away with the profits and left the debt on the table. Few noticed as long as builders were throwing up homes whose prices kept rising each year. Then reality arrived.

Those dreamy sub-prime mortgages were converted into real-life debt a year or two later with suddenly inflated monthly payments that buyers couldn't meet—even when the mortgages were stretched over forty-year terms. Homeowners began walking away from houses they couldn't afford, and within months the market was flooded with homes nobody wanted, deflating prices everywhere.

---

2 A Ponzi scheme involves paying abnormally high returns to early investors out of the money paid in by subsequent investors. The perpetuation of the high returns that a Ponzi scheme advertises (and pays) requires an ever-increasing flow of money from investors in order to keep the scheme going. The scheme is named after Charles Ponzi, who employed the technique after emigrating from Italy to the United States in 1903. As simple and obvious as it may appear, the concept keeps appearing today, usually as part of an overall investment fraud.

Meanwhile, Wall Street was finding ever more obscure ways to make money out of nothing. Some created hedge funds. If you expect the economy to move generally upward over time, you may choose to invest in a mutual fund. If you are unsure about the future being bright, you could choose a hedge fund, which works by assuming things are going to hell or somewhere in that vicinity. But while mutual funds are available to anyone with cash, most hedge funds are sold only to those with *mucho dinero* to invest and enough savvy to understand the risks involved. If you don't have at least a million loonies in your sock drawer or elsewhere, hedge funds aren't interested in you.

A hedge fund can profit from bad times through short selling—borrowing shares in a publicly traded company, selling the shares immediately, buying the shares back when their price has dropped as predicted, returning the shares to their owner along with an interest payment, and pocketing the profit.

Hedge funds grew enormously in recent years, reaching an estimated $2 trillion in value by 2007. Controlling that much of the market gave hedge fund managers an enormous amount of market clout, a fact made more disturbing when you remember that hedge fund managers are seeking profit from failure, not success. This did not disturb the regulators because nothing existed to warn about the danger of so many people having so much power to influence so many companies. Besides, the kids were alone in the candy store, remember?

INSURANCE PEOPLE WHO COULDN'T COVER THEIR OWN RISK

Over at AIG, the world's largest insurance company and the eighteenth-biggest corporation in all the world, they were hatching their own profit-producing offspring. Why subsist on premiums from millions of grubby little home and automobile owners, the AIG brain trust asked, when people down the Street were making billions via the stock market? This was a game the AIG brass wanted into, and they bought their way to the table with credit default swaps, or CDSs.

CDSs were insurance policies sold to companies trading in corporate bonds. "If you own $100 million in corporate bonds," the AIG salespeople said, going door to door on Wall Street, "why not buy a little insurance in case the corporation can't come up with the cash when the bond is due?" If the corporation issuing the bond lacked the cash to meet its IOUs and the investor had purchased insurance on the investments from AIG, AIG would cover the loss.

The idea scored well with many investors. It scored exceptionally well with hedge fund managers, who saw credit default swaps as a means not of covering their bets but of making sure their bets paid off. Remember that hedge fund managers earn their keep only when things go bad. Remember as well that financial and investment mavens are related to the guy who sets up a table on Main Street, hides a pea under one of three walnut shells, moves the shells around and bets you can't find it. Follow the damn pea all you want, but it will never be under the shell you choose.

Clever hedge fund managers realized that purchasing a credit default swap indicated that someone had determined that the company to whom the swap applied was in trouble financially. Buying a multitude of swaps on a company's bond issue would signal concerns about the firm's financial viability and, in turn, deflate the value of its stock. Deflated stock prices make money for hedge fund managers. Almost overnight, hedge funds were purchasing swaps on companies that initially had no financial problems yet found their share price sliding into the cellar. By the end of 2007 AIG held $562 billion in credit default swaps on its books.

Since those 562 billion greenbacks represented half of AIG's total assets, you might expect the firm's top brass to hedge against their own loss. If you do, you are smarter than the celebrated brain trust at the insurance company, because they didn't. And when the short sellers won by depressing the stock prices and the companies lost because they couldn't meet their bond payments, the grease was under AIG's feet.

Why didn't anyone at AIG, or anywhere else, see this possibility and act on it? Because the enormous amount of money flowing into AIG as CDS premiums blinded them to the risk. Until the spigot turned off in 2005, AIG earned an estimated $6 billion in CDS premiums, of which about 20 per cent went to the crew managing the CDS unit. Everyone should have a chance to get rich if they choose, but by any measure these profits bordered on the obscene.

The frantic dancing continued until mid-2007, when a few observers noted that areas of the United States, especially California, Arizona and Nevada in the Southwest, which had profited most from the sub-prime mortgages, were beginning to look like ghost towns. Homes were being abandoned and/or repossessed, and housing prices began sliding down the other side of the mountain when more and more owners, faced with sudden jumps in their mortgage payments, walked away from their dream castles. Financial insiders began quietly disposing of their ABCP investments, passing them on to people who did not realize that the bubble had begun to burst. One report claims that senior traders at Goldman Sachs pocketed $2 billion in profits earned by other people's misery before the full extent of the housing collapse became apparent.

Panic spread through the industry like spilled Scotch on satin sheets. Individuals and corporations started cashing in their ABCP investments, or tried to. By now, U.S.-bred ABCP was scattered literally around the world. The French bank BNP Paribas, which had peddled ABCP investments through its mutual funds, was forced to suspend the funds and cease payments to investors until it could place a true value on the ABCP in its portfolio. A couple of German banks followed suit, soon joined by some U.K. banks and building societies. Panic ensued.

In the summer of 2007, someone calculated that ABCP investments were linked to about $32 billion in bad American housing loans and mortgages, much of it uncollectible. The estimate was far off the mark. As a measure of the magnitude of this current crisis, $32 billion sounds almost like a reasonable number now.

Bit by bit, the crack in the dam containing an enormous flood of mismanaged investments began to widen.

BAD NEWS TRAVELS FAST . . . AND FAR

Anyone who believes that nothing threatens the speed of light for velocity is unfamiliar with international banking when it comes to sharing bad news. Almost overnight, banks around the world lost trust first in their own ABCP holdings and later in the ability of other banks to meet their debt obligations. In those circumstances, a bank's best move is to hoard its cash, refusing to pass it on to other banks whose financial foundations might be shakier than their own.

The flow of money between banks froze solid. Money no longer moved easily in the form of loans and credit, stifling businesses that cannot operate efficiently on a cash-only basis. Banking, the third Baron Rothschild said, consists "essentially of facilitating the movement of money from Point A, where it is, to Point B, where it is needed." But money was no longer moving easily, and the process of banking almost ceased.

Through the balance of 2007 and the summer of 2008, the entire structure began to crumble despite claims by U.S. president George W. Bush and Canadian prime minister Stephen Harper that their respective countries' economies were "in good shape."

Entities managed by people who for years had publicly decried any oversight by governments under any circumstances realized their nether parts were in an ever-tightening wringer and turned to governments, whimpering for help in the form of taxpayer money. Fannie Mae, Freddie Mac, AIG, major investment banks and others were the first to arrive hat in hand, followed later by the Big Three automotive companies. The world was facing something more than a recession and, we hope, something less than a depression.

Canada enjoyed shelter from the worst of the collapse, at least at the beginning. ABCP and hedge funds were never as widespread in our financial industry as in the United States and elsewhere, although by the end of 2008 the federal government was being asked to contribute as much as C$5 billion in assistance to ABCP holders. We were also blessed with commodities such as oil, wheat and nickel as well as other sources of income. Canada was not immune, however. Globalization links industrialized countries around the world like one giant charm bracelet, and all of us began following the United States into the same dark, deep sinkhole. By November 2008, the International Monetary Fund estimated, worldwide losses triggered by ABCP and other shenanigans had reached almost US$1.5 trillion, and before things settled, banks around the world would lose US$10 trillion in assets.

In 2009 we are witnessing not one crisis but a blend of linked financial crises, each creating problems for the others. They include:

- global credit paralysis based on a weakening of trust between international financial groups
- a global recession in which every industrialized nation's economy is shrinking in size and strength
- the world's largest auto industry teetering on the brink of bankruptcy

- record deficits and enormous debt, which, along with the challenge of fighting two distant wars, threaten the stability of the world's biggest economy

It's not far-fetched to view this as a fundamental breakdown of the entire financial system, global in scope and massive in scale, involving every aspect of finance and investment—every stock market, every issuer of bonds, the insurance and real estate industries, major manufacturing sectors and commodities from potash to petroleum.

In the words of the Columbia University economist Frederic Mishkin, "This shock is in many ways more complex and harder to deal with than the financial shock that occurred during the Great Depression."

How far will we fall? No one knows for sure yet. But falling we are. In the last four months of 2008 the Toronto Stock Exchange (TSX) lost almost 50 per cent of its value. Unemployment shot upward even as Ottawa politicians acted like kindergartners sticking out their tongues at each other instead of grappling with the problem.

We need answers and ideas. And that's what follows.

“Wal-Mart has replaced General Motors as the largest employer in America with over 1 million employees where, instead of earning a middle-class wage, workers earn starvation wages of $13,861 a year—a salary that is below the poverty line. Meanwhile, four out of the top ten richest people in America are relatives of Sam Walton, Wal-Mart's founder, and are worth over $100 billion.”

U.S. CONGRESSIONAL REPRESENTATIVE
BERNIE SANDERS, FEBRUARY 2004

Q: How can the problems of big international banks and insurance companies have a negative effect on me?

A: Banks don't merely lend money to you and your neighbours. They loan and borrow money, sometimes overnight, to and from other banks around the world. These short-term borrowings are used to make long-term loans to you, me and business clients. Thus, a bank may grant loans of several million dollars extending over years, yet have the funds to cover these commitments on hand only until the weekend (you cannot try this at home).

Sounds risky? *Pas de sweat.* Bankers were always confident that new short-term sources of cash would appear when needed, and that's what usually happened under normal circumstances. Banks earn a profit through short-term borrowing at low interest rates while granting long-term loans to customers at a higher interest rate. Those of us who don't toil among the vaults and boardrooms of major banks are rarely, if ever, aware of this constant flow of credit, just as we're not normally aware of the blood flowing through our arteries and veins until a disaster occurs. Then we bleed, as the banks did in late 2008.

Until the summer of 2008, banks charged each other a minuscule 0.08 per cent or so above the bank rate when making loans to each other. When Canada's bank rate was set at 2.5 per cent annually, this meant that Scotiabank, for example, could tap BMO Bank of Montreal for a few hundred million loonies and pay a mere annualized rate of about 2.6 per cent for the privilege. The loss of trust, especially between international banks, created a sudden leap in these interest rates. By the end of September 2008 some banks in Europe were desperate enough to pay 11 per cent annual interest for overnight loans, and were finding no lenders.

On an international scale, banks began keeping their money away from each other and from all but their best customers. Businesses needing loans to purchase raw materials or new equipment, or hire more staff, found the banks tight-fisted. Expansion stopped, companies downsized, and a wider economic avalanche began.

The banks and their dilemma represented only one corner of the crisis. AIG, headquartered in New York, is one of the most international of companies, operating in 130 countries. Until it sought bailout assistance from Washington, AIG claimed assets of about $1 trillion. When the economic situation worsened through 2008, many companies whose bonds AIG had covered through credit default swaps were unable to meet their obligations and AIG had to pay up big time.

This is the disaster that essentially sank the world's largest insurance firm—not a natural event like a hurricane or earthquake, but a mad pursuit for profit that ignored the scope of the risk and the possible consequences.

“The meek shall inherit the earth.
But not the mineral rights.”

J. PAUL GETTY,
AMERICAN OIL MAGNATE

Q: Who is to blame for this disaster?

A: There is plenty of blame to go around, and plenty of places to put it.

U.S. banks, regulators and successive federal governments can be blamed for encouraging greed to override good sense. Twisting, extending and breaking long-established rules about creditworthiness, down payment requirements, debtor obligations (in the United States, homeowners can walk away from their mortgaged property, leaving the mess for the lender to clean up; in Canada, the owner remains responsible for losses) and other guidelines created a housing boom, followed by a housing bubble that burst with a world-shattering pop. The uninhibited and uncontrolled denizens of Wall Street and elsewhere compounded the situation with new and complex derivatives that few people understood but many wanted, based on their attractive earnings and the high marks awarded them by ratings agencies. Governments and regulators maintained a hands-off approach, believing in the power of market forces and due diligence by investors to avoid a general collapse.

Incorrect assumptions were made by many people in many locations at many levels. Assigning guilt may be satisfying to some degree, but it will not restore losses or rebuild fractured economies.

Instead of constantly looking back, we should be looking ahead. Which admittedly can be a little frightening at this point.

“A few words about our economy, our economic fundamentals. They are rock solid.”

CANADIAN FEDERAL
MINISTER OF FINANCE
JIM FLAHERTY,
MAY 24, 2006

Q: Are we sliding into another Great Depression?

A: The good news is, No. Or probably not.

Among the differences between this crisis and the depression of the 1930s is the original source of each event. In 1929, the disaster began in the stock market, which had been outrageously overpriced for some time and was poised for a major correction. Many individual stock portfolios had been assembled on margin—the purchaser/investor paid only a fraction of the amount needed to buy the shares, borrowing the balance from banks or brokers who held the shares as security. When stock prices started tumbling, the banks demanded the balance owing, forcing investors to sell their shares to cover their debts. These sales depressed stock prices even further, causing problems for new investors. Soon everyone was desperately selling stock, driving prices downward into a death spiral. A run on the banks began, with depositors frantically withdrawing their savings, leaving the banks that survived (many did not) with little money on hand and even less inclination to loan it.

The current financial crisis began not in the stock market but in the banks themselves, and while we may not know precisely what to do now, we know what *not* to do, based on the experience of the 1930s.

For the first few years of the Great Depression, governments did nothing to replenish a shrinking supply of money. From 1929 to 1933, the available money supply worldwide shrank by 33 per cent while the U.S. government basically stood around and watched.

The most significant action taken by the U.S. government was to pass the Smoot-Hawley Act, which also happened to be the dumbest move. Smoot-Hawley effectively killed international trade by imposing high tariffs on twenty thousand products imported into the United States. In retaliation other countries, Canada among them, imposed similar tariffs on American goods and products, and within two years of its passage Smoot-Hawley had reduced the country's international trade by 66 per cent, deepening the crisis even further. Nobody anywhere in the world wants anything like another Smoot-Hawley.

One measure of the Great Depression's disastrous impact is the reduction in a country's gross domestic product, or GDP, the total value of all goods and services produced in one year. In the years from 1929 to 1933, Canada's GDP dropped an average of more than 10 per cent annually, an enormous amount. During the same period, the U.S. economy shrank by more than 45 per cent.

Nothing on that scale appears to be happening now, nor is it likely to occur. Things are bad, but not as bad as they were in our grandparents' time.

Q: Couldn't the experts see this coming?

A: Some did. Unfortunately, the people who could act on their warnings chose to do nothing. This includes leading politicians in Canada and the United States, along with gurus such as Alan Greenspan, former chairman of the U.S. Federal Reserve, and top executives at investment banks up and down Wall Street.

Martin Wolf, a columnist for the *Financial Times* of London, wrote in February 2008, "America's economy risks the mother of all economic meltdowns." Few people listened to him, despite the fact that he was an experienced and otherwise widely respected economist.

He wasn't alone. Nouriel Roubini, professor of economics at New York University, predicted the recession in 2006 and listed twelve steps that would lead to it, all of them kicked off by the worst housing recession in American history and losses of $300 billion in sub-prime mortgages. According to Roubini, these and other events led to steps 10 (a major collapse in stock prices), 11 (a "drying up" of credit and liquidity) and finally 12 (a vicious circle of losses, capital reduction... and fire sales of assets at below fundamental prices). Many observers tagged Roubini a pessimist and a worrywart, suggesting everybody should keep the party going. Two years later, they were forced to admit that Roubini had seen the future, and it was not working.

No one, including politicians, wanted to face reality. In April 2008, President George W. Bush declared, "The U.S. economy is dynamic, resilient and responsive." And in October 2008, Canadian prime minister Stephen Harper, in the midst of a federal election, kept repeating a similar mantra: "The Canadian economy is strong." Instead of looking more deeply into disturbing evidence of escalating mortgage foreclosures in the United States, questionable ABCP values and overextended credit arrangements, free-market advocates pointed to low interest rates, low inflation and stable growth. Only when it was too late to avoid the credit crunch and the resultant crash did they suggest the party might be over.

Politicians and denizens of the investment community prefer to avoid delivering bad news to voters and investors, but they faced the music eventually. Even Alan Greenspan, whose platitudes had dispelled concerns about the American economy for years, found himself cornered in a congressional meeting room where he admitted, "Those of us who have looked to the self-interest of lending institutions to protect shareholders' equity—myself especially—are in a state of shocked disbelief." Later he agreed that it had been an error to oppose regulating the sale and management of derivatives, acknowledging that financial institutions didn't protect shareholders and investments as well as he expected.

“This is far and away the strongest global economy I’ve seen in my business lifetime.”

U.S. TREASURY SECRETARY
HENRY PAULSON,
AUGUST 8, 2007

Q: Is technology to blame?

A: To a degree, yes. But computers did not make the decisions that led to the current disaster. People driven by greed and dreams of glory are the real culprits.

Banks and investment houses may have tested the viability and risk factors of ABCP and other instruments with computer modelling, but the programs chosen to crunch this data used information extending back only to the mid-1990s. It appears that nothing in these programs, or in the minds of those who created them, accounted for the possibility of a dramatic drop in house prices. In most of North America, housing prices had been rising for almost half a century, and the risk of them dropping off by 25 per cent or more within a short period of time seemed unlikely. Not aware of this possibility, the programs delivered a more optimistic range of possibilities than was warranted.

Computers also fostered the evolution of complex derivatives without exploring all their implications. The financial wizards who created and marketed these products were not interested in implications. They were interested only in profits. To put it bluntly, the computers could figure out the mechanics of many derivatives but the people who created and marketed them could not.

Other factors played roles that we are only now beginning to understand, and the impact they made will be felt for years to come. Here's an example: In 1978, financial services in the United States and Canada represented about 11 per cent of each country's GDP. This includes the activities of banks, brokers, investment houses, mutual funds and dozens of other services dedicated to turning one pile of money into a bigger pile of money. By 2008 these same operations generated 21 per cent of the GDP. In contrast, manufacturing activities in the United States and Canada accounted for 25 per cent of GDP in 1978. Thirty years later the proportion had shrunk to 13 per cent.

Ask any economist about the relative benefits of an economy based on manipulating money versus one creating valued goods out of raw materials, and the answer will always favour manufacturing. Producing hard goods continues to represent, along with a viable agricultural industry, the backbone of a prosperous industrialized nation. Financial services should be an adjunct to manufacturing, never a replacement. Yet since 1978, North America has jettisoned its manufacturing base in favour of services, most of them financial.

“There have been transactions that would have been unheard of five years ago, where major firms with hundreds of thousands of transactions a day have given up exchange operations and gone to a third party to handle execution and order flow. There are no boundaries anymore on where economic sense drives change.”

JOSEPH ANASTASIO,
EXECUTIVE VICE PRESIDENT,
CAPCO FINANCIAL SERVICES CONSULTANTS,
NOVEMBER 14, 2005

Q: How are our leaders dealing with the situation?

A: Governments are addressing two prime issues: *solvency* and *liquidity*. To a lesser extent they are dealing with the third leg on this wobbly economic stool, which is confidence. These are being handled rather differently in Canada than elsewhere.

Solvency involves the ability of banks to pay their bills. With so many losses caused by ABCP, banks around the world are having difficulty laying their hands on cash to meet even their most basic obligations. As explained earlier, this is a relatively minor concern in Canada because our good old tight-fisted major banks tended to avoid ABCP and other toxic derivatives. Bank losses have been considerable—all of the five major banks wrote off hundreds of millions of dollars through 2008—but our banks have more than enough equity to handle them. In fact RBC Royal Bank, Canada's largest bank, managed to turn a $1-billion profit in the third quarter of 2008 and continued paying dividends. We may pause here to reconsider our complaints about bank fees and congratulate our bankers on their wisdom.

Liquidity—access to money needed to keep businesses operating—is another matter. Even in Canada, banks are hoarding cash because they are unsure which of their customers will be able to pay them back. Governments have responded with a drop in interest rates and verbal assurances that our money is safe in domestic banks.

Reducing already low interest rates is an effective method of stimulating the economy, but it has its limits. In the 1990s, facing a national housing and liquidity crisis similar to our current international situation, Japan cut interest rates to absolute zero. The impact on the problem proved negligible. Even interest-free loans weren't sufficient to kick-start the Japanese economy, and there is no assurance that this move alone will be successful now for us and the rest of the world. The United States and Europe realize they are running out of room to move in encouraging an economic revival driven by low interest rates.

Canada, in the opinion of many observers, is in a unique position and may warrant a different solution.

For example, 70 per cent of the U.S. GDP is derived from consumer spending, so America depends on its citizens to shop their way out of the problem. In Canada, only 55 per cent of GDP depends on consumer spending. Thus, tax cuts and rebates would not have a similar effect here. Instead, the January 2009 federal budget focused much of its effort on infrastructure projects and stimulating businesses to expand and hire more staff, or at least minimize layoffs, while calming the nerves of the rest of us with retraining programs, an extension of EI benefits, and modest income tax reductions.

Projecting deficits over the next two years of $60 to $70 billion, Ottawa predicts the recovery from this mess will put us back in the black within five years. Very nice, except the assurance comes from the same people who boasted about the strength of our economy less than six months earlier.

Let's all try to be just as optimistic and a little more realistic.

Q: How much can we count on President Obama to fix things?

A: During the run-up to the 2008 U.S. presidential election, it became clear that Americans were ahead of the presidential candidates when it came to the economy. Early in the campaign, Republican nominee John McCain famously declared that he had little knowledge and less interest in economics, and Barack Obama, for all of his emphasis on the need for change, rarely addressed the scope of the economic situation in detail or suggested any hard solutions. Yet on election day seven out of ten Americans identified the state of the economy as their prime concern.

While possessing an admirable background in academe and law, Obama has little training or experience in economics. On its own, this is secondary to the economic expertise of his advisers. If he chooses them wisely and listens carefully to their counsel—including those whose views he may disagree with, a talent not evident in the case of his predecessor—he may justify the hope and trust that the rest of the world has bestowed upon him.

Even if President Obama submits and implements effective policies, it may be some time before the world is prepared to grant the United States the same leadership role in economics and other activities that it has enjoyed for the last several decades.

“Last Friday we learned that our economy has now had 52 months of uninterrupted job growth. That's a record. That's the longest period of job creation on record. Our entrepreneurs are taking risks. Our small businesses are expanding.”

U.S. PRESIDENT
GEORGE W. BUSH,
JANUARY 10, 2008

Q: What are other countries doing?

A: Nothing is more illustrative of the seriousness of the situation than the response of the U.S. government. Long declared the last bastion of free enterprise, the United States has been forced to effectively nationalize several privately operated organizations. These include the major mortgage lenders Freddie Mac and Fannie Mae along with AIG, which now operates within the secure embrace of the federal government.

If nothing else, the U.S. government is insisting on flexibility in its decision making. In November 2008 U.S. treasury secretary Henry Paulson changed his mind about that $700-billion TARP, initially targeted to purchase mortgage-related assets. Instead, Paulson directed the funds toward replenishing the cash position of major banks and extending consumer credit opportunities. These steps are similar to those taken by the United Kingdom and other countries, but whereas other countries offered the banks cash as an option, the nine leading American banks had no choice. They were told to accept the cash and the government monitoring of their activities that came with it.

At year's end, the U.S. Federal Reserve reduced its key interest rate to a range between 0 per cent and 0.25 per cent, lowering the prime rate that banks charge on loans to their customers. The move was more psychological than practical because, first, it represented an admission of the failure of other steps the Fed had taken in response to the crisis; second, it left no room to move in the future (you cannot go lower than zero); and, third, most Americans didn't want to borrow money—they wanted to pay off their debts and hold on to any cash they had.

More important moves were taking place on the international front. There's nothing like a shared crisis to persuade countries to set aside their squabbles and join forces to a limited extent. Working within organizations such as the European Central Bank, the International Monetary Fund and the Bank for

International Settlements, Western industrialized nations began looking for ways to generally, if not universally, coordinate their actions. Now and then a rebel appeared, such as Ireland, which, departing from the herd, promised all depositors in Irish banks a full guarantee on the safety of their money. This triggered a sudden flow of cash into Irish banks and nasty words from other countries. Ireland didn't care. It was looking out for itself and its people first.

China responded to the crisis by implementing actions almost identical to those taken by the United States and Europe. In addition to increasing the volume of money circulating within the country by 17 per cent, Chinese leaders promised to increase the amount of money made available to its leading banks by 100 billion yuan, or US$14.6 billion. These actions were taken after a summit meeting involving the leaders of China, Japan and South Korea. All three countries agreed to take similar actions with the goal of strengthening the world economy.

India, the other Asian tiger, responded in similar fashion, injecting about US$4 billion into the country's economy. India's economy was predicted to grow at "only" 7 per cent in the year ending March 2009 and slow to "a mere" 6 per cent the year following. This kind of growth in Canada or the United States would be considered explosive, but both levels pale in comparison with the more than 9 per cent annual growth in the Indian economy over the previous three fiscal years. Not all is so rosy, however. By the end of 2008 the value of India's stock market had fallen more than 50 per cent.

Q: What steps are being taken to prevent this happening again?

A: Very few. While countries claim to be tightening their restrictions on financial activities within their own borders, the bigger question of controlling international movement of currencies by private organizations is unlikely to be addressed.

Thanks to instant communication and fund transfer technology, finance is now the largest and most globalized sector of the world economy. In terms of speed, size and impact nothing compares with the ability of money to move literally at the speed of light from one location in the world to another location, free of government oversight. Nations are reluctant to restrict the movement of money for fear of having their banks and financial industry cut off from access to investment funds. Imagine one blackjack dealer in a Las Vegas casino insisting on knowing the identity and financial status of every player at the table before the cards are dealt. For various reasons, gamblers would choose other tables to play their game. Convert the blackjack tables into industrialized countries and you can understand why they all want to be equally attractive to folks with money to spend.

There's a problem here, however. As the events of the past year have demonstrated, the world of international finance is inherently unstable. Unfounded rumours, big-time speculators, overly aggressive bankers, obscure financial derivatives and a hundred other factors can affect the global money markets in dozens of ways, most of them unpredictable and unfortunate. The system cries out for stability.

One solution would be to appoint a global financial regulator, a Super Alan Greenspan (but with substantially greater perception and awareness) assigned to either permit or prohibit certain financial transactions between countries. You may expect this to happen in the foreseeable future. You may also expect to win the Lotto 6/49 this coming weekend. The odds are roughly similar.

So we are left with an immensely influential system that wobbles, stumbles and surges of its own accord generally free of regulation, subject to only mild supervision by a disparate group of managers whose prime loyalty is to the interests of their own country or state.

The International Monetary Fund (IMF) was created in 1944 to provide stability to the industry, but it has been left far behind by technology and the growth of global financial markets. Its rarely expressed support of government intervention to stabilize the economy is anathema to the free-market advocates who have influenced monetary decisions in the United States and the United Kingdom over the past quarter-century. The IMF is like a referee at a professional wrestling match whom everybody ignores.

The IMF will not be granted wider powers, nor will a new structure emerge to wield authority over international finance because no political leader dares suggest trading his or her country's sovereignty for stable international financial operations. That's why international finance is free to operate in the fashion of the Wild West rather than as a disciplined organization whose goals extend beyond this month's profit statement. The dream of countries agreeing to submit to controls over the flow of capital between all nations will remain just that—a dream.

Perhaps the best solution is to treat global finance and its contagious risks in the same manner in which concerned citizens in enlightened nations are treating environmental challenges: think globally and act locally.

In this case, "locally" means exercising caution about personal investments and debts, and supporting governments that promise effective regulation of financial operations within their own borders.

Let's remember that this entire situation is the product of the boom-and-bust cycle of a free economy, and that the "boom" side frequently expands into a bubble. Bubbles rarely subside quietly; they tend to burst with disastrous results. The history of Western civilization abounds with similar incidents, many based on seemingly illogical premises.

In the seventeenth century, Holland experienced a tulip mania that defied all common sense and led to economic downfall for thousands of families. The entire country went mad for exotic tulips, and when speculators entered the market, bidding on future prices for tulips to be distributed the following spring, a single tulip bulb rose in price until it exceeded twenty times a worker's annual income. People purchased bulbs at higher and higher prices, intending to resell them for a profit. When some citizens succeeded in marketing their futures and pocketing a fat profit, others jumped on the bandwagon in hysterical greed. The scheme, of course, depended on someone willing to pay the high prices and take possession of the bulbs, and when tulip traders could no longer find new buyers, the demand for tulips collapsed, prices plummeted and the speculative bubble burst.

Almost a century later the South Sea Company, a British corporation, was granted exclusive rights to conduct trade with South America, most of it involving slaves. Following a public offering of shares, their price climbed more than ten times their initial value, once again driven by public mania, before the process collapsed and threw thousands into the poorhouse. Reportedly the brilliant Isaac Newton lost £20,000 in the scheme, and later he lamented that he could measure the speed of the planets but could not calculate the madness of the people.

More recent bubbles include the stock market crash of 1929 and the bursting of the dot-com bubble in 2001.

These and other events should serve to generate sober second thoughts among future investors and speculators. Unfortunately, when bubbles begin to expand, memories among those seeking to profit from them appear to shrink.

Q: What happened to Iceland? How can an entire country go broke?

A: During the past ten or fifteen years, there were worse places to be than Iceland, from an economic perspective. Unemployment was low, Icelanders earned more than the average European income, foreign money financed investments in energy resources and aluminum smelting, and the country's exports rose steadily in value. By 2005 Iceland was assessed as one of the world's wealthiest countries on a per capita basis.

The events of 2007–2008, however, may become a future textbook lesson in national economic catastrophe, because without the drastic and unprecedented steps taken by its European neighbours, Iceland could have become literally bankrupt—a country whose banks, government and citizens were all flat broke.

Here is how it happened.

In the 1980s, Iceland began restructuring itself from a tiny isolated country dependent on fishing into a vibrant nation actively involved in technological developments.

The efforts paid off. Iceland evolved into the fourth most productive country in the world, based on GDP per capita. With unemployment below 1 per cent and its economy growing 5 per cent annually, Iceland could claim that its government's policies were simultaneously prudent and successful. The country was committed to limiting foreign borrowing, controlling inflation, diversifying the economy and privatizing state-owned businesses.

Iceland established a business-oriented environment, becoming fifth in the world according to the Index of Economic Freedom in 2006 while boasting one of the world's lowest corporate tax rates and banks that operated with minimal government regulation. Which led to the nation's economic downfall.

The three Icelandic banks sent several young future financial stars to New York and London for training, and they returned bursting with enthusiasm to convert their homeland into Wall Street North, or at least a land known more for its financial power than for its fishing fleet.

Inspired by visions of grandeur from the new generation of bankers, the banks aggressively pursued almost any investment opportunity that floated their way. They built an investment treasure chest by borrowing first from the country's well-funded national pension plan, and turning later to the international money market. Impressed by their visions if not by their experience, international sources advanced billions of dollars to the Icelanders, creating substantial debt for the banks' customers and shareholders.

Knowing their own citizens could never provide sufficient capital from retail deposits to play with the big boys in New York and London, the banks turned to the Internet to tap a wider source of cash. It was both a stroke of genius and a flight of folly. Online banking, the Icelanders advertised, cut their costs so much that they could offer exceptionally high interest rates to people from Detroit to Dubai who sent cash to Reykjavik. (Let's be honest—why else would you send money to Iceland?)

Money flowed in from everywhere, attracted by the high interest offered to depositors. With full pockets, the hell-for-leather Icelandic banking honchos made highly leveraged investments in foreign markets. Kaupthing, the leading Icelandic bank, even purchased the U.K. merchant bank Singer & Friedlander for more than C$1 billion.

Icelanders, who for years had been compared to Canadians when it came to conservative saving and spending habits, grew giddy with their new-found wealth. Thanks to higher interest paid to depositors by Icelandic banks, the country's currency soared in value, reducing the cost of imports and inspiring a credit-driven consumer spending spree. By 2007 Icelanders had amassed debts that were more than twice their disposable income. And the band played on.

The Icelandic Young Turks, believing the good times would last forever, borrowed and invested in a manic display of national pride and private greed. By 2008, when the mackerel hit the fan via the global credit crunch, the banks were told to pay up. But they couldn't. Their leveraged investments had collapsed, leaving an aggregate debt of all three Icelandic banks estimated at *six times the country's gross domestic product.* In Canadian terms, this would be like Canada's major chartered banks owing $7.2 trillion, most of it to foreign banks and investors.

The banks could no longer meet their obligations, no one wanted to own an Icelandic krona, interest rates on credit balances shot to 18 per cent or more, pension funds collapsed, and the entire country shuffled to the European Union (EU) and the International Monetary Fund (IMF), where it held out its cap and asked for spare change. By the end of 2008, the country remained 4 billion euros short of the amount it required to claim solvency. Foreigners who had sent money to the three

Icelandic banks via the Internet clamoured to retrieve deposits estimated at US$8.2 billion, about half the size of the country's entire economy. They may never see a penny of it.

Iceland represents something of a test-tube experiment in which aggressive bankers weaned on Wall Street ambition with access to international funding opportunities were permitted to foist their own view of reality—*the party's just getting started!*—on an entire nation. Whenever a hint of such unbridled exuberance appears in future years, let's hope that someone sits down and reads all the gory details of this unfortunate fiasco.

Iceland may be the most notable country to tumble from wealthy and exalted status to the international equivalent of a homeless street person, but it's not alone. For 25 years Ireland exceeded every other country in its economic growth, earning the title of Celtic Tiger. Its economy roared past those of most other countries in the world on a wave of cutting-edge technology, thanks to heavy investments by firms such as Intel, Yahoo, Adobe, Microsoft, HP, Apple, Google and others.

Things have changed. The Irish economy shrank dramatically in 2008 and will continue to stumble through 2009. Tax revenues have collapsed and the 2009 budget deficit is expected to hit 7 per cent of GDP.

Ireland's crisis is substantially different from Iceland's train wreck, although both were triggered by the global credit crunch. In Ireland's case, the country hitched its economic well-being to a vastly inflated housing bubble and its reliance on U.S.-based investments. Irish exports to the United States rose steadily throughout the 1990s and by 2007 accounted for more than a fifth of all its international trade. In 2008 the Emerald Isle counted 620 American subsidiaries in Ireland (employing 100,000 people, or about 5 per cent of the workforce) while the United States generated at least one-third of offshore investment in Irish manufacturing. When the American economy turned inward, money ceased flowing into Ireland, which had few cushions to soften the blow.

The world indeed has grown smaller and more closely linked. We are all in the same boat in many ways, and when the boat begins leaking we all risk sinking.

Q: Now that everybody agrees we're in a serious recession, how long will it last?

A: It's a logical question that unfortunately cannot be answered.

Some economists claim that the swift action taken by the United States and other countries to inject cash into their economies derailed a much more serious recession. Once liquidity and confidence return to the marketplace, the optimists suggest, the world will witness a slow and steady return to reasonable economic health. While they admit that the North American automotive market is in shambles, they claim a pent-up demand for new cars will cause a spurt in this sector within two or three years. They also look beyond North

America for silver linings, noting that the enormous consumer markets of India and China will not be denied their expansion and will soon resume major purchases of commodities such as base metals, food, minerals and petroleum.

Others are more pessimistic. China and India, they suggest, are not immune to the economic infection. Both countries boast dynamic economies but they have already begun to suffer the effects of sharply reduced consumption. While they can boast lower costs and (in China's case) enormous reserves of foreign currency, China and India are far less stable than their Western customers. Conflicts between India and Pakistan, horrifically demonstrated by the terrorist attacks in Mumbai in November 2008, may yet lead to open warfare. China's political system, a patchwork of authoritarian Communism and laissez-faire capitalism, is basically unstable, and a sharp drop in employment within the country could trigger waves of unrest, preventing the government from dealing effectively with economic challenges.

Pessimists also point to Japan's experience in the early 1990s, when credit dried up in a manner similar to the process that has led to the current global situation. Despite the Japanese government's best efforts, the country's economy remained stagnant for fifteen years and Japan now boasts a deficit equal to 1.5 times its GDP—an astonishing burden that may hamper Japan's economic performance for decades.

And back in the United States, where the housing bubble first grew and then burst, a second wave and even a third one of mortgage foreclosures are expected between 2009 and 2011 when the artificially low interest rates are reset to levels that homeowners cannot afford.

Canada will no doubt feel the ripple effect of these and other waves, but our reserve of natural resources may enable us to avoid a serious case of the Japanese Disease. Or perhaps not. The truth is that nobody knows for sure.

“With investment in industry and agriculture yielding low profits owing to overcapacity, large amounts of surplus funds are circulating and being invested and reinvested in the financial sector. The financial sector has turned in on itself.”

UNIVERSITY OF THE PHILIPPINES PROFESSOR WALDEN BELLO, SEPTEMBER 2008

Q: Some people are warning of "deflation." Should I be worried?

A: Yes and no. Deflation is a serious phenomenon that can lead to financial disaster. Fortunately, it also appears unlikely to occur in full force.

Inflation has been defined as "too much money chasing too few goods." By contrast, deflation is "not enough money chasing too many goods." With inflation, prices rise across the board, dragging wages and salaries with them. With deflation, prices drop, and keep dropping. You may think lower prices represent a Good Thing. They do not. They represent disaster.

When the prices of products and services continue to fall over a long period, consumers delay making purchases because they expect to pay less for the same product or service in the near future. Nobody goes shopping, which means fewer people go to work, creating large segments of the population that have no money to make a purchase at any price, high or low. Reduced demand sends prices even lower and the spiral continues.

A deflationary spiral spreads disaster everywhere. Those with cash on hand abandon any thoughts of investing it. Cash becomes ever more scarce in the marketplace, driving prices ever lower. Property values decline but debt remains static. When homeowners discover the value of their residence is less than the balance of their mortgage, they abandon any effort to repay it even if they are still employed.

While deflation was a characteristic of the Great Depression, it is not likely to occur under current conditions. Governments are printing all the money they need, which normally creates an inflationary climate, not deflation, and the prices of major commodities such as petroleum and gold, while fluctuating widely, are generally moving upward. All of these run counter to a deflationary spiral. Of course, this crisis has fooled a number of people who underestimated its depth.

We all have much to worry about, including the possibility of widespread unemployment, a wave of bankruptcies among businesses and private citizens, and high levels of inflation based on those government printing presses working overtime to print more money. These dangers are real; the risk of severe deflation remains speculative.

Q: I keep hearing about "strong" and "weak" currencies. What's the difference, which term fits the loonie, and why should I care?

A: Currencies become strong when their value rises against the value of other currencies. A weak currency is one whose value falls compared with others.

In 2002 you could purchase a loonie for about 60 cents in American change. Five years later, the same purchase would have cost you about $1.10 in Yankee currency, but by late 2008 the loonie had slid back to less than 80 cents American.

The fluctuations were caused by a number of factors, including speculation. On currency markets, the loonie is just another commodity like rice, wheat and pork bellies. Speculators watch hundreds of different factors in countries around the world, determine the future impact on their currencies and buy or sell accordingly. Political turmoil, changes in international trade agreements, climate-related impacts on agricultural production, national strikes and an untold number of other incidents, real or anticipated, influence the belief that a country can meet its international financial obligations. The country's currency floats or sinks according to these perceptions.

Interest rate levels are another critical factor, and one that governments can control. Raising Canada's bank rate above the norm attracts international investors who like the idea of parking their cash in a place that pays higher interest. An increase of even a quarter of a percentage point (0.25 per cent) is often enough for Big Money to begin transferring cash into Canadian coffers. Before it can, however, foreign currency must be converted into Canadian dollars, so Big Money goes shopping. When Big Money starts buying up loonies by the hundreds of millions, the demand for our currency rises and our dollar shows its muscle.

Similarly, when the world wants to buy Canadian goods and resources, it needs first to acquire Canadian dollars, and currency markets respond in the same way. The jump in the value of the Canadian dollar from 2005 to 2007 was powered primarily by the world's demand for our resources.

What goes up always comes down eventually. Demand for Canadian resources such as potash, nickel and petroleum began to wane in 2007; when fewer people need our goods, fewer people want our money, and the loonie's value slid with the reduced demand. All in all, it pays a country to maintain the strength of its currency within certain limits.

As a major global trader, Canada tends to prosper when its dollar is somewhat lower than the reserve currency, i.e., the U.S. dollar. (The Canadian dollar is considered a benchmark currency, employed to judge the overall health of the American dollar. Other benchmark currencies include the Hong Kong dollar, the Australian dollar, the Swiss franc, the Japanese yen and the euro.) A strong currency generally signals widespread confidence in that country's economy and political stability.

Opinions vary, but Canadian economists generally prefer the Canadian dollar to hover around 85 cents in U.S. currency. That's strong enough to keep imported goods at an affordable price and "weak" enough to make our goods and services attractive on the international market.

“A man without money moves quickly through the marketplace.”

ARAB PROVERB

Q: Who is John Maynard Keynes and why are so many people talking about him?

A: Keynes was a British economist who rose to prominence in the midst of the Great Depression. Keynes proposed that instead of leaving markets alone to settle their difficulties via simple supply and demand mechanisms, the state should play an active role in managing its economy. Governments, he suggested, can stimulate economic growth and improve stability of a capitalist society through adjustments in taxation and interest rates and by financing public projects.

Until Keynes put forward these ideas, classical economists believed that all markets were self-correcting. If the price of a product or service rose too high, demand would drop until the price was reduced to an acceptable level, when demand would resume. Keynes rejected this concept where serious recessions were concerned, declaring that renewed demand would be insufficient to lift the economy back to health within an acceptable period of time.

It can all get very complex and depressing (which is why economics has been called "the dismal science"), but Keynes's central position was based on the proposition that governments should provide equilibrium to an ailing economy, cooling it down with interest rate hikes when things grow too hot and boosting it with interest rate reductions and public spending when the economy becomes too sluggish. The latter prescription included the suggestion that in treating a recession, governments should spend more money than they generate through taxation, creating a deficit. Deficits, Keynes lectured, were not necessarily a bad thing.

From 1940 to 1980, Keynesian economics were adopted by much of the industrialized world. With the arrival of Reaganism in the United States and Thatcherism in the United Kingdom, the prevailing philosophy turned against Keynes; opinion leaders insisted that governments should stay out of the way of business and avoid deficits under any circumstances. Within a few years Keynes's ideas became as out of date as spats and corsets.

To disciples of Reagan and Thatcher, Keynes sounded suspiciously like a socialist, especially with his belief that government policy should direct money toward those at the lower end of the income spectrum during difficult economic times. This group, Keynes suggested, would be most likely to spend money on needed goods and services, lifting the overall economy.

Reagan and Thatcher took the entirely opposite view. You don't give breaks or cash to the lower classes, they lectured. You give them to the upper classes, and watch their expenditures trickle down to the great unwashed. What's more, governments should never interfere in the mechanics of business and finance under any circumstances. All markets are self-correcting, and every new regulation represents a barrier to the creation of wider wealth.

It's impossible to avoid the notion that the Reagan-Thatcher economic philosophy is responsible for the current financial crisis. Certainly the idea that any regulation of financial transactions is too much regulation helped justify some of the Wall Street excesses discussed earlier.

In any event, John Maynard Keynes's ideas have been resurrected from the trash bin and reinstalled, especially in the United States, where his name was often spoken with the same derision reserved for Marx, Engels and Castro. In 2007, the Bush administration issued cheques to every U.S. citizen with orders to spend the money and kick-start the slowing economy—a classic Keynesian response. Now governments around the world are planning extensive public projects, directed to rebuilding infrastructure and injecting wages and salaries into the economy via government spending. Nobody appears worried about deficits anymore.

Somewhere, John Maynard Keynes is smiling.

“The sky is still there, the sun is coming up every day and the Canadian economy is still functioning. We started from a very strong starting point. Individual Canadians and businesses are going to go out and make decisions and see opportunity and take advantage of those opportunities.”

BANK OF CANADA GOVERNOR
MARK CARNEY,
OCTOBER 23, 2008

Q: What will be the long-term effects of this crisis?

A: The world was never the same after the Great Depression, and the impact of this crisis will be similar, without doubt.

Over the last quarter-century, markets triumphed over governments in the industrialized world. In some ways, this was a positive change; through the 1970s businesses such as energy, communications and transportation found themselves restricted by often nonsensical government regulations. Airlines in Canada had to ask permission from a federal ministry to fly passengers to destinations outside the country, and the sole provider of telephone communications in Canada could not alter its rates or aspects of its service without government approval.

The swing away from excessive regulation really began with the Reagan-Thatcher years in the United States and the United Kingdom, gaining momentum when Canada and other countries followed suit. Pendulums swing, and you may have noticed that they never stop in the middle; they move as far past the centre as their momentum can carry them. That's what happened with the deregulation wave. Now it's time for the pendulum to swing back toward the boring but comfortable middle, and we will see the results in three ways.

First, expect the introduction of regulations into each country's financial markets. This has already begun in the United States. No one in Congress is giving AIG, the surviving investment banks and the individual retail banks hundreds of billions of dollars without insisting on attaching a few conditions, such as that they account for every taxpayer dollar they spend. The banks have to follow strict rules set by the federal government, which will become, in effect, a senior business partner to them all.

Similar steps are being taken in other countries. Some of the tightest regulations will likely be applied to the players in the credit derivatives market—those clever souls who fashioned swaps, ABCP and other creatures that few people truly understood but many believed would prove profitable. The appeal of credit derivatives was enormous; by 2008 the market for them represented $55 trillion in cash, despite a structure so complex and obscure they made quantum physics look like a game of checkers.

Next, regulatory measures are likely to extend beyond financial activities. Expect many countries to prevent uninhibited market forces from dictating the price of commodities, especially food. Sudden inexplicable upsurges in food prices generated riots in many countries such as India in early 2008. Investigations traced the increase to international speculators. In response, various developing countries banned food exports and restricted trading in futures associated with the industry. Trade restrictions are not generally a wise move, but this was probably unavoidable. We can only hope that similar restrictions with the potential to harm Canada will be minimal.

Finally, we may be about to enter a dramatic new era in which the economic clout, intellectual authority and moral leadership of the United States becomes diminished. Emerging economies such as China, India, Indonesia and others, along with South Korea and Brazil, are beginning to shape the international financial agenda. With its massive stock of U.S. bonds, China effectively holds the trump card when it comes to influencing many American decisions. This situation was set up over the years of the George W. Bush presidency, which burned its way through an enormous amount of international goodwill following 9/11. The incredibly profligate spending of the Bush administration transferred hundreds of billions of U.S. dollars into foreign hands while creating a national debt of a size that boggles the mind. Other countries watched in dismay, recognizing that this financial ball and chain would restrict U.S. power in several unpredictable ways in the future.

As China's vice-premier Wang Qishan lectured his American counterparts at a Sino-American summit in late 2008, "The teachers now have some problems."

“I have found a flaw.”

ALAN GREENSPAN,
FORMER CHAIRMAN
OF THE UNITED STATES
FEDERAL RESERVE BOARD,
COMMENTING ON HIS
LONG-HELD SUPPORT
FOR TOTAL DEREGULATION
OF THE FINANCIAL INDUSTRY,
OCTOBER 23, 2008

Q: How have Canadian banks come out of this?

A: In better shape than the banks of most other countries.

In 2008, the World Economic Forum ranked Canada's banking system the best in the world. Since 1940, only two regional banks have failed in Canada, yet more than forty American banks have gone under since 2000.

Canadian banks operate in a different environment than banks in the United States, where, surprisingly, banks are subject to much tighter regulations. Historically, the American philosophy favoured small locally owned banks with few branches, creating a highly competitive but unstable system leading to the collapse of thousands of banks over the past century. Free of these restrictions, Canadian banks expanded nationally, producing a broader and more stable foundation that allowed them to ride out difficult times.

They also reflect the unique character of Canadians when it comes to banking. We are risk-averse and heavily insured, and we tend to save more of our earnings than Americans. This makes us ideal clients for banks, who don't need to engage in high-risk activities to generate greater returns for us. Example: Few residential loans in Canada are securitized. Most are on the banks' balance sheets, where they can be tracked and assessed.

What's more, Canada's banks tend to be more focussed on their operations from the top down. Many of the largest American banks function as part of holding companies whose CEOs are removed from many day-to-day operations. Massive Citibank is owned by Citigroup, which describes itself as "the world's largest financial services organization," and banking remains only part of its corporate activities. When the subprime mortgage disaster struck in 2007, top executives at Citigroup claimed not to fully understand ABCP and the various derivatives and had no idea of Citibank's exposure to them. The degree of exposure became apparent with the realization that Citibank had lost between $8 billion and $11 billion as a result of the subprime catastrophe.

Under the Bank Act, Canadian banks are the only institutions allowed to hold and enforce mortgages, and outside firms are prohibited from purchasing large batches of mortgages and selling them for a profit—the root of the sub-prime problem. Still, a few ABCP batches found their way across the border. Most Canadian banks sniffed at them, didn't like the aroma and walked away. According to claims made by Canaccord and its clients over ABCP losses, Scotiabank did not walk away until its investment banking and capital markets unit, Scotia Capital, had wholesaled a batch of ABCP accounts to Canaccord. Scotiabank, Canaccord alleged, had received "materially relevant information... on the risk associated with U.S. subprime exposure" yet continued to pocket substantial commissions even as the ABCP morphed into a galaxy of financial black holes.

CIBC bought into some ABCP based on sub-prime mortgages, registering a C$2-billion loss and costing the CEO of CIBC World Markets and his chief risk officer their jobs. Otherwise, the exposure of the Canadian banks to ABCP remains substantially less than in the United States and many European countries.

Along with the wariness of the major Canadian banks, we can also acknowledge the prudence of large insurance companies and other substantial pools of capital, including Great-West Life, Brookfield Asset Management and Quebec's Caisse de Dépôt. The Ontario Teachers' Pension Plan juggles well over $100 billion in investments.

In roaring good times, these operations and their managers are often criticized for being overly cautious. At the moment, they are being praised for their discretion. They may also be closer to their customers, especially the Canadian banks. Most major American banks draw only 10 to 20 per cent of their income from personal or retail banking—folks who use the bank for their chequing and savings accounts. The overwhelming majority of their profit is earned from institutional clients, while Canadian banks remain more attuned to and reliant upon their retail operations.

It appears that the rescue packages and interest rate manipulations applied in the United States, Canada and elsewhere have worked to preserve the financial stability of the banks. Their ATMs continue to spew out cash, and no depositors have lined up to withdraw their savings in a panic, in contrast to the darkest years of the Great Depression.

So there is no reason to be concerned about the viability of Canada's banks. With total assets of about $2.5 trillion, the largest five Canadian banks are consistently rated by *Forbes* magazine among the top two hundred banks in the world. The current crisis may see them growing even stronger and more secure, thanks to expansion in the United States, where they are acquiring troubled financial institutions. TD Bank Financial Group already operates the largest discount brokerage in the United States as well as a chain of well-managed bank branches. BMO Financial Group owns Harris Bank, a highly regarded Chicago-based bank with almost three hundred branches across the U.S. Midwest, and Scotiabank represents a banking power throughout the Caribbean and South America.

In November 2008, a Toronto-based financial commentator travelling to New York noted that her flight was "crammed with Canadian mergers and acquisitions lawyers and other investment specialists, travelling to Manhattan to pick over the corpses."

Q: How far will the value of my house fall?

A: It depends on the same factor that dictated much of the original value of your home: location.

According to the Canadian Real Estate Association, the price of existing residential properties across Canada in October 2008 had fallen an average of 10 per cent compared with October 2007. The difference varied widely according to location: prices in Quebec remained virtually unchanged while those in Newfoundland actually rose.

Remember, however, that housing prices in many areas of the country had been artificially high for a few years, creating our own domestic housing bubble. A correction was not only expected, it was virtually necessary. In time, housing values will resume their rise based upon factors such as regional economics and mortgage rates. To whatever extent they are adjusted, Canadian house prices are unlikely to suffer the degree of precipitous plunge experienced by the United States because our housing bubble wasn't nearly as large.

The differences between Canada and the United States are dramatic. Ours is a cyclical correction; theirs is a virtual meltdown. Our banks have mortgage money to lend; theirs are either strapped for funds or practising extreme caution.

If you're comfortably settled in your home, with or without a mortgage, the current price fluctuation should have little impact on your lifestyle, assuming, of course, that you remain employed and able to meet your mortgage payments.

Here's another angle: Housing prices in many regions of Canada had risen so high that many young families with limited income had begun abandoning their dream of becoming homeowners. The price readjustment, combined with low mortgage interest rates, may make home ownership a more realistic dream for them.

If the value of your house has dropped, this reduces your overall equity position somewhat. But unless you are using the equity in your home to leverage investments or are tapping it to cover other expenses—not a good idea for the most part—this is a loss whose pain you are unlikely to suffer.

Q: How safe is my job?

A: Not nearly as safe as it was a year ago.

Corporations under financial pressure look around for the most efficient way of cutting costs, and the most immediate answer is found as soon as the executives step out of their office suites. Do we really need all these people? executives ask themselves.

In any recession period, some jobs are safer than others, and a few companies actually thrive on conditions that look grim to others.

Public sector jobs, especially at the provincial and federal levels, appear to be safe. Governments do not want to appear to be contributing to the economic challenges by dumping workers on the street, and an expansion in publicly funded programs may actually inspire a hiring wave by government to administer these programs.

Depending upon your profession and point of view, you will be either pleased or appalled to learn that lawyers may benefit because of the legal actions launched and defended by corporations trying to deal with the crisis. Bankruptcies demand legal action, and lawsuits are certain to appear based on failure to meet contractual and financial obligations.

You might also consider sending your resumé to companies dealing in liquidated goods, buying inventory and fixtures from companies that cannot survive the recession.

A more practical small step: update your resumé, and keep a few copies on hand in case they're needed.

“The financial crisis has become an economic crisis, and the world is entering an economic period unlike, and potentially as dangerous as, anything we have faced since 1929.”

CANADIAN PRIME MINISTER
STEPHEN HARPER,
NOVEMBER 22, 2008

Q: What will happen with the stock market?

A: It depends on how you look at it.

In the long term—over the next five to ten years—it will rise, perhaps passing the peak established in the summer of 2008 when the TSX nudged 15,000. One senior economist at a major Canadian chartered bank claimed that in "only a typically paced recovery, benchmarked to past cyclical yardsticks," the TSX could climb to 12,000 sometime during 2009. On the other side of the fence Eric Sprott, a highly regarded investment fund manager who had been warning about the risk of the current crisis for years, suggested we are in a mini-depression, facing years of recovery.

In the short term—meaning the next six to twelve months—the market will likely take investors on an extended roller-coaster ride, climbing to inspiring heights one day and plunging to demoralizing losses the next. This extreme volatility will be welcomed by a few hardened investors who move in and out of the stock market with all the grace and success of Wayne Gretzky weaving his way through a pickup hockey game on a frozen pond. Assuming you lack Gretzky-like skills, stay on the sidelines. Eventually things will begin to settle down and you will feel free to move into the market with well-considered (or well-advised) purchases of quality blue-chip stocks.

Timing, of course, is everything, and the major winners will buy their stocks at the dismal bottom. No one can predict when this will be reached. Best suggestion: don't try to time the market for maximum returns. When it appears that things are getting better, you may pick up some stock bargains and ride them up.

If you are concerned about the equity portion of your RRSP/RRIF—the amount invested in publicly traded shares and equity-based mutual funds—the past year or so has probably felt like an extended root canal procedure. Losses of 50 per cent or more in these sectors kicked the foundation out from the plans of many people who will be retiring soon.

Which leads us to the next question.

“Looking back on it, it was madness.”

JOHN VARLEY, GROUP CHIEF EXECUTIVE OF BARCLAYS BANK UK, ON THE POLICY OF BRITISH BANKS TO LOAN 125 PER CENT OF RESIDENTIAL PROPERTY VALUES, DECEMBER 15, 2008

Q: The value of my RRSP has dropped through the floor. Will it ever recover?

A: Stock market values have fallen more than 40 per cent in Canada and other countries since their peak in the summer of 2008. At least as much as any indicator, this demonstrates the seriousness of our current situation. If your RRSP is heavily invested in stocks, its worth has probably declined by about half the same proportion. If you suffer from heart problems of any kind, opening your monthly statement is not advisable.

Before sinking into a well of despair, however, consider these points. They may not represent light at the end of the tunnel, but they could shine a little glow of comfort and understanding on your plight.

Some sectors of the market may never recover. It's too soon to tell, for example, about stocks related to the automotive industry. If nothing else, this proves the wisdom of diversification—spreading the equity portion of your RRSP across several different industries.

If you haven't sold your stocks or equity-based mutual funds yet, don't. Assuming your RRSP investments consist of shares in quality companies or units in well-managed mutual funds, so far your loss is on paper. Selling your shares or fund units crystallizes your losses, meaning they become real and likely irrecoverable. No one knows where the bottom of the market is, but we're surely close enough at this point to wait for a recovery.

The markets may have fallen more than 40 per cent, but the overall economy has not. Stock markets are driven by two factors, fear and greed. Neither is rational. Greed drives the market higher than it's worth because everyone wants to board a bandwagon. Fear drives the market lower than necessary because it generates a cycle of selling that plunges prices lower, creating anxiety in a new crowd who decide they want out, and away we go.

Many people who follow the stock market minute by minute are already purchasing undervalued shares in certain companies, expecting to earn substantial profits when the market turns around. It will, and they will. Where did they get the cash to buy these shares? They sold stock when the market was flying too high. They remembered the story of Icarus, and knew the wings would soon fall off.

Should you begin buying stocks at their current distressed prices? The short answer is "Yes." If you truly want to restore your RRSP's value, don't be a wallflower.

There are two good reasons for entering the market now. First, the market always anticipates both good and bad developments. Prices fell well ahead of the recession and will rise in advance of the recovery. They may not have hit rock-bottom yet but they are close enough for even cautious investors to move in and pick up bargains. Second, tens of billions of RRSP dollars are in money market funds or short-term bonds earning less than 2 per cent a year, meaning they're not invested, they're parked. Eventually a geyser of money will return to the market, pushing prices to excessive levels. You can wait for the crowd or you can anticipate it. Anticipation is preferable.

Your best bet: Indexed Exchange Traded Funds (ETFs) from Barclays or one of the major banks. Mirroring benchmarks by Standard & Poor's or the TSX, these funds are inexpensive to manage, so you keep more earnings for yourself, and they can be traded like common shares. Choose funds based on the TSX Composite Index, Large Capitalization Index, the Financial

Index and, if you believe oil prices will rise to $100 a barrel, the Energy Index.

Now you can appreciate the value of guaranteed bonds. Astute investors and their advisers have long preached the wisdom of using bonds guaranteed by provincial or federal governments as a foundation for an RRSP. In recent years, the earnings from these investments have been less than impressive—barely 4 or 5 per cent annually. They have held their value, however, as the stock market crumbled around them, and that's the solid foundation that every RRSP needs. In fact, if 100 per cent of your RRSP consisted of short-term (less than five years to maturity) government-guaranteed bonds, the value of your plan has probably risen because investors everywhere have been dumping their stocks to buy these secure bonds, driving their prices up.

When things settle down, review the structure of your RRSP according to this simple formula: the percentage of your RRSP invested in government-guaranteed bonds, T-bills or short-term GICs from a major bank should equal your age. At age fifty, this means half of your RRSP should be in boring bonds that don't make a lot of money but help you sleep at night.

If you can afford to make an RRSP contribution, do so. The benefits of a tax deduction are still there, and we all appreciate the importance of saving for the future. Entering the equity market at this stage may prove a bonanza over the next five to ten years because even the best-quality stocks are considered underpriced. Don't, however, make a decision in this area without seeking advice from a trusted and qualified investment counsellor.

Q: The rules say I must withdraw a minimum percentage from my RRIF. This seems unfair given its sharply decreased value. What's happening to help me out?

A: Once you convert your RRSP to a Registered Retirement Income Fund (RRIF), which must happen the year you turn seventy-one, you are required to withdraw a minimum percentage of your fund based on its value at January 1 of that year. The minimum withdrawal percentage rises with each passing year. At age seventy-one, only 7.38 per cent must be withdrawn. By age ninety-four, the minimum withdrawal is

20 per cent of the RRIF value. All withdrawals, of course, are subject to income tax.

If your RRIF balance on January 1 in the year you turn seventy-one is $300,000, you are required to withdraw at least $22,140 (7.38 per cent of $300,000) whether you need it or not. To RRIF owners who do not need the money, this is a bad deal. A RRIF may have been valued at $300,000 on January 1, 2008, but by the end of the year it may have declined to $200,000 or less, thanks to the drop in stock market prices. According to the original rules, the RRIF owner must still pull $22,140 out of the account even though this could represent more than 10 per cent of the actual balance.

Ottawa rode to the rescue by reducing the minimum withdrawal amount by 25 per cent for the 2008 taxation year. On that basis, seventy-one-year-old RRIF owners needed to withdraw a minimum of 5.535 per cent. Those who withdrew more than the new minimum could return the difference to the RRIF and deduct this amount from their 2008 taxable income, up to March 1, 2009.

This policy may or may not be extended depending upon stock market performance, so watch for future announcements from the Canada Revenue Agency and the Ministry of Finance.

Q: Could the Big Three automakers go broke, and should I care?

A: They could and you should.

While the automotive manufacturing sector is admittedly centred in Ontario and, to a lesser extent, Quebec, it represents so much of this country's industrial wealth and activity that its demise would affect Canadians from St. John's to Victoria. Injecting about $28 billion into the national economy each year, the industry supports more than 500,000 workers including those employed by parts manufacturers, dealerships and peripheral services. You cannot yank that much income generation from an economy and eject that many people from well-paying jobs without the entire country feeling the jolt.

Many people feel little sympathy for the industry and its workers, claiming the vehicles produced by GM, Ford and Chrysler were shoddily designed and assembled by overpaid union auto workers. Although the Big Three made errors in the past, such as placing more emphasis on SUVs and pickup trucks than on fuel-efficient cars for urban needs, these "errors" served a ready market. General Motors, for example, made an estimated $12,000 profit for every Hummer that rolled off its lines, and pocketed barely a tenth of that amount for each compact car it sold. From a purely business standpoint, it made sense to build and sell those behemoths as long as people lined up, cash in hand, to purchase them. Unionized auto workers sought a piece of the profitable action.

Jolting change arrived in the form of sharp increases in gasoline prices through 2008 and the growing appeal of hybrid vehicles, most of them Japanese imports. In the midst of this came the credit crunch. The sharp drop in auto and truck purchases across North America sent GM, Ford and Chrysler to the brink.

A substantial number of Canadians and Americans proposed a hands-off approach to the ailing domestic industry. "Let the Big Three slide into bankruptcy protection like other companies and they'll become leaner and better managed without tapping into taxpayer funds," they proclaimed. Many cited the experience of Air Canada, which sought bankruptcy protection in 2003 and five years later was rated among the economically healthiest of the world's airlines. But an airline's commitment to its passengers ends when they step safely off the plane at their chosen destination. An automobile company's commitment can extend for years via warranty and service arrangements. Who would spend thousands of dollars on a car whose manufacturer may not be around to service it in the future?

The "Let 'em die on the vine" attitude toward auto manufacturers may also demonstrate a bias against blue-collar working people. After all, governments quickly stepped in to assist the financial and investment industry—the origin of the entire mess—with hundreds of billions of dollars in loan guarantees and assistance. Are traders, dealers, brokers, MBAs and hustlers on Bay Street and Wall Street more entitled to sympathy and support than the greased-to-the-elbows workers at auto and auto parts plants scattered across central Canada?

The situation with automakers is as much political as it is economic. The U.S.-Canada Autopact of 1965 integrated the automobile manufacturing industries of both countries and delivered widespread benefits for everyone. (The pact was abolished in 2001 because of a ruling by the World Trade Organization.) While Canada accounts for perhaps 10 per cent of the North American auto market, until 2008 Canadian auto plants manufactured about 23 per cent of the vehicles produced on the continent.

As long as the industry was healthy, this was a non-issue to the United States. When the Big Three executives went to the U.S. Congress seeking financial assistance, Americans expected their taxpayer dollars to be spent exclusively in that country. To complicate things, representatives of American states without a Big Three presence queried why their constituents should underwrite the jobs of workers in Michigan, Ohio and Indiana. The prospect of U.S. government officials agreeing to finance the Canadian arm of the industry is less than nil, leaving the task up to Canadian taxpayers, voters and auto customers.

Canada, like the rest of the industrialized world, is muddling through an enormous crisis that will surely change the face of our economy all across the country, not just in central Canada where the assembly plants are located. Unless no alternative exists, the loss of the auto industry and its resulting impact on nearly half a million Canadian homes represents collateral damage that must be avoided.

Q: Why are many people promoting gold as an investment?

A: You don't carry gold in your wallet or purse to buy goods and services. You carry pieces of paper and bits of steel and copper whose value is based on a promise.

For thousands of years, people did not pay each other for goods and services with promises. They paid each other with pieces of gold and silver. These metals conveyed tangible worth no matter whose name was on the coins. In times of political or economic uncertainty, people turn to gold until things settle down. Through all the changes humanity has endured since Biblical times, this sentiment remains unchanged in much of the world.

A new element has been tossed into the quest for gold. The people of China and India value gold as a display of wealth and success, and as security in difficult economic times. Even though both countries are expected to feel the impact of the credit crunch, this attitude is unlikely to change. In fact, any available extra money may be spent on gold. The supply of gold, like the supply of petroleum, is dwindling, however, and reduced supply combined with rising demand is expected to boost the price upward.

Gold enjoys attractive benefits for investors, including the fact that ownership involves no trust in the liability of others. Even if you stuff your mattress with paper money, you're trusting the Bank of Canada to make good on its promise to support every loonie in your Sealy Posturepedic. Gold carries no such liabilities—you own it, you control it.

All of these factors pushed the price of gold above US$1,000 per ounce momentarily in early October 2008 when the true scope of the economic crisis first became apparent. Within a few weeks the price had fallen back to around $700.

This demonstrates one of gold's less attractive qualities for small investors. The gold market is very volatile, even over short periods of time. Other drawbacks: gold does not pay dividends like quality stocks, and you can't walk, swim or boat on it as you can with real estate.

Balancing these disadvantages is the historical and cultural perception of gold as protection against economic disaster; it may not pay dividends, but its value will never drop to absolute zero cither.

Should you consider purchasing gold? Some advocates of investing in gold predict its price will zoom well beyond US$1,000 per ounce within the next year or two in step with rising inflation. Or it may not. If the ups and downs of the economy have made you and your RRSP nauseous, consider investing a portion of your account in quality gold stocks to help ride out future volatility.

“If the market crashes, the authorities are going to pour so much money into the system to try to avert economic disaster. Money has to go somewhere. Some of it will go to gold. If the gold price heads higher, you've got the cheapest gold stocks in history.”

JOHN EMBRY,
CHIEF INVESTMENT STRATEGIST,
SPROTT ASSET MANAGEMENT,
SEPTEMBER 12, 2008

Q: How will the crunch affect my credit card debt?

A: It's another good news/bad news situation.

Good news: Interest rates for valued customers of chartered banks and other institutions are dropping, in line with reductions in the rates charged by the Bank of Canada. At the end of 2008, the federal bank's rate descended to 1.5 per cent annually, a level not seen for more than fifty years. The banks followed suit, although they did not immediately match the reduction. Still, interest rate bargains could be found. A few credit card providers, such as Capital One, offered a three-year guaranteed interest rate on unpaid balances (for top-rated customers only) of just 5.8 per cent annually. And if you owned a floating-rate mortgage, your monthly payments were reduced noticeably.

Bad news: Where banks, credit cards and other lending institutions are concerned, the world is now populated with either heroes or deadbeats. Heroes are long-time customers with a steady income and a record of paying their bills on time. They are rewarded with reduced interest rates, although the amount of credit they can access may be reduced. Everyone else is a deadbeat, punished with hikes on the interest charged on unpaid credit balances.

In late 2008, TD Canada Trust announced that TD Visa credit card owners who delayed making minimum payments on their balance past the end of the thirty-day billing period would see their annual interest leap five full percentage points to 24.75 per cent, more than four times the rate enjoyed by Capital One's most valued customers.

Even if you qualify for rates as low as those proffered by Capital One, now is not the time to load your credit card with unnecessary purchases.

“I’ve never seen such uncertainty in terms of looking forward to the future. I’m very worried about the Canadian economy.”

PRIME MINISTER
STEPHEN HARPER,
DECEMBER 15, 2008

Q: What became of global warming, the last crisis before this one?

A: The world may have to abandon plans to address this problem for a while.

The current state of affairs represents a political challenge as much as an economic one. Earlier, we noted that the prospect of countries agreeing to apply tough regulations on international financial transactions was highly unlikely. The probability of governments dedicating a substantial portion of their energy and national assets to the global warming crisis appears just about as weak.

Governments may have to choose between lending support to social programs that will provide citizens with some degree of security and funding items such as wind generators and solar panels as a means of reducing fossil fuel emissions. Wind generators and solar panels, you may have noticed, do not vote.

Even projects that do not require dipping into national coffers will be postponed. Several European countries, for example, had planned to impose severe restrictions on heavy carbon-producing industries such as iron and steel manufacturing. When all the countries were united in this strategy, it appeared viable. Now each country is looking inward at its own shaky economy and reconsidering the move. If one country should waive such restrictions it could be enough to attract new or expanded industries in an environment where expensive steps to limit emissions are not necessary. Everyone wants to encourage industrial development now, and any move that could be construed as anti-industry becomes suspect.

As part of their efforts to rebuild their infrastructure, however, countries could initiate new renewable energy projects, reducing their carbon footprint by an impressive measure. And reduced economic activity has already produced noticeable reductions in carbon emissions from industries and automobiles.

Q: If this too shall pass, what's the long-term outlook for Canada?

A: At the risk of sounding like a Pollyanna, the answer is, Good. Or at least, not bad compared with other countries.

One reason for this positive outlook is the basis of our economy. Like it or not, we remain very much a country based on commodities and resources. Our manufacturing capacity has shrunk and may continue shrinking, which is disturbing in many ways. But we continue to produce wheat, nickel, gold, potash, lumber and other materials the world requires. And despite the move to electric and hybrid vehicles, the world will require a substantial volume of petroleum products for the next several generations. If the companies mining the Alberta oil sands can solve the concerns of environmentalists and world petroleum prices return to more than US$100 per barrel, they will continue to generate wealth and income at an impressive rate.

Another reason for looking ahead with optimism is our traditional boring and conservative style of muddling through. As much as we may grumble about political flapdoodle, bureaucratic inefficiency and maddening inefficiencies, things are better economically in Canada than almost anywhere else. Standard & Poor's predicts that sovereign ratings—essentially the credit ratings of entire countries—will decline over the next several decades. The sovereign rating for the United States in 2005 was AAA, the very highest; S&P expects it to decline to BBB by 2020 and down to non-investment grade by 2030, when other countries including France, Italy, Japan and Korea will join it. Things get worse. By 2040 the sovereign ratings of all countries except one will have declined to non-investment grade.

The sole exception? Canada, whose current AAA rating will have been reduced to a still respectable and attractive AA.[3]

---

3 As much as this sounds like a P.R. release from a promotional arm of the Canadian government, the source is quite legitimate and respected. The details are found in "Financial Risk Management: Lessons from the Current Crisis... So Far," December 4, 2008, Knowledge@SMU (Singapore Management University), http://knowledge.smu.edu.sg/.

This won't refill your RRSP or ensure your job security at the moment, but it may keep your blood pressure low and minimize the furrows in your brow.

AND IN CONCLUSION

It's the economy falling, not the sky

Most of us like to believe we can make logical decisions if we are provided with hard facts and competent advice. The year 2009 brought plenty of both. Unfortunately, the facts were depressing and the advice was bewildering.

Example: In November 2008 the chief portfolio strategist of TD Waterhouse predicted the TSX index would break 12,000 by the summer of 2009. Meanwhile, a senior economist with Merrill Lynch called for Canadian stocks to barely keep their tails above 8,000 for the entire year. This should not be a surprise, because both predictions were spawned by people who either did not see the crash coming or saw it and refused to sound the alarm.

Throughout this book I have attempted to provide hard facts without jargon, noting that we are witnessing not a reprise of the Great Depression or the end of civilization but the latest in a perpetual cycle of booms and busts, bubbles and crevasses, joy and despair. This downturn is more disturbing than others because of its width, affecting virtually every industrialized nation, and its depth, altering forever the foundations of the Wall Street–centred investment community.

Like other periods of slower economic activity it will be painful for some, challenging to most and profitable to a few. And (count on this) it will end. Until it does, I suggest you remain skeptical of anyone who claims to know exactly when.

John Lawrence Reynolds
January 2009

Glossary

ASSET-BACKED COMMERCIAL PAPER (ABCP)
Securities with a supposedly predictable income stream based on "bundles" of different assets including subprime mortgages, car loans and credit card loans. By combining different types of underlying loans, ABCP was presumed to deliver high interest over short terms (thirty to sixty days) at low risk.

BONDS
IOUs made more complex by time. Most corporate and government bonds extend as far as thirty years into the future, paying a fixed rate of interest until their maturity date. The interest is earned by clipping coupons from the bonds and exchanging them for cash. Canadian government bonds, both federal and provincial, are considered the safest of all available investments.

COLLATERALIZED DEBT OBLIGATIONS (CDOs)

A type of asset-backed security and structured credit product constructed from a portfolio of assets. The mix included relatively secure components, medium-risk or "mezzanine" elements and higher-risk equity-based portions.

CDOs were traded from 2000 to 2008 between financial institutions, some of which lacked the will or competence to monitor credit performance and cash flows. Many CDO products were listed on balance sheets on a "mark to market" basis (see page 133). When credit markets became paralyzed in 2007, the liquidity of CDOs became questionable and the market for them vanished, adding to the general loss of confidence among banks and other lending agencies.

CREDIT DEFAULT SWAPS (CDSs)

A complex derivative that functioned as an insurance policy purchased by a bondholder. The owner of the bond paid a premium in exchange for a guarantee that, if the issuer of the bond fails to pay the bond's full value at maturity, the issuer of the swap would pay the amount owing. AIG, the world's largest insurance company by far, issued swaps worth hundreds of billions of dollars between 2000 and 2008.

DEFLATION

Wide reduction in prices, values and incomes as a result of a moribund economy. The last deflation period was the Great Depression of 1930 to 1938.

DERIVATIVE

Any security whose value is based on (derived from) another underlying security. Most derivatives are similar to side bets on the future value of a commodity such as oil, gold or pork bellies. Derivatives enable large profits to be made with relatively small upfront investment.

EQUITY

The value of everything an individual, corporation or other entity owns after all the liabilities are deducted. If your home is worth $350,000 and your mortgage balance is $150,000, you have $200,000 in home equity. If your mortgage exceeds the value of your home, you have negative equity.

FINANCIAL INSTRUMENT

Any legal obligation of one party to transfer something of value—usually cash—to a second party at some future date in exchange for an acquired product or service. Bonds and cheques are simple financial instruments.

GROSS DOMESTIC PRODUCT (GDP)

The total value of all goods and services produced in a calendar or fiscal year by a sovereign nation, employed as a measure of the size of the country's economy. Canada's GDP in 2006 was $1.178 trillion.

HEDGE FUND

Aggressively managed mutual fund designed to generate high returns through the use of sophisticated financial strategies including derivatives, short selling and leveraged trading in domestic and international markets. Because of the substantial risk involved in hedge funds, access to them is usually restricted to individuals with high net worth who supposedly comprehend the risk involved and can afford to absorb anticipated losses.

INFLATION

Too much money chasing too few goods, causing prices and wages to rise in dramatic fashion. During the two decades from 1988 to 2008, inflation in Canada has been held to an acceptable 2 to 3 per cent annually.

LEVERAGED INVESTING

The act of borrowing money to increase the potential profit of an investment such as shares of common stock. Borrowing money from the broker selling the shares is called buying on margin.

For example, an investor with $1,000 can purchase 100 shares priced at $10 per share. If and when the share price rises to $15 per share, the investor can sell the shares and make a gross profit of $500. By borrowing $9,000 to add to the original amount, the investor can purchase 1,000 shares at $10 per share. If the shares rise to $15 each, the investor pockets a gross profit of $5,000 less interest owed on the borrowed $9,000.

The opportunity of multiplying the anticipated profit is balanced by the amplified risk of loss. In the example above, if the $10 stock falls to $5, the investor loses substantially more than the $1,000 originally intended for investment.

LIQUIDITY

The ability of an asset to be easily converted to another asset according to its owner's preference without causing a significant movement in its price and with minimum loss of value. Money, or cash on hand, is the most liquid asset because it can purchase any other asset of equal value. A home is a substantially less liquid asset because an appropriate purchaser must be found, price and terms must be negotiated, and various collateral expenses must be accounted for. Shares in a publicly traded company are less liquid than cash and more liquid, generally speaking, than real estate, although both are subject to wide swings in market valuation.

Liquidity also refers to the ability of a business to meet its payment obligations by possessing sufficient liquid assets.

MARK TO MARKET

An accounting method of assigning a value to a financial instrument based on its current market price. For example, if an investor owns 100 shares of a stock purchased at $40 per share and the stock now trades at $60, the "mark-to-market" value of the shares is 100 shares at $60 each, or $6,000. The true value can, and frequently does, change overnight, but the mark-to-market figure remains fixed, creating an unrealistic perception of its actual worth. Conservative accounting principles rely upon book value, which is the actual price paid for the shares.

MONEY MARKETS

Generally open only to banks and major financial institutions, these are locations or arrangements in which substantial funds are borrowed or loaned for short periods ranging from thirty days to one year. Small investors participate in money markets through mutual funds.

PREFERRED SHARES

Shares in a publicly traded corporation whose owners receive a fixed dividend before other profits are distributed as dividends to holders of common shares. In exchange for the assured dividend, owners of preferred shares usually enjoy no voting rights.

RECESSION

A reduction in economic activity for two consecutive quarters. Severe drops in economic activity extending across several quarters (or years) may be termed a depression, although no widely accepted definition exists.

SECURITIES

A transferable certificate of ownership, such as common or preferred shares in a corporation, bonds, mortgages and similar instruments.

SHORT SELLING

The practice of seeking to make a profit from anticipated reductions in the value of a security, usually common shares of publicly traded companies. A short seller borrows shares from their owner, paying a small interest rate to hold them for a fixed period of time. The shares are sold immediately at the current market price. If the short seller is correct in anticipating a drop in value, the shares can be purchased at a lower price within the period agreed upon with the owner. The owner takes back the shares plus interest, and the short seller keeps the profit based on the difference between the share prices for the two transactions. Of course, if the share price increases during the agreed-upon period, the short seller loses.

Short selling is a risky strategy, often employed by hedge fund managers.

SUB-PRIME MORTGAGES

Mortgages on residential property issued by lenders to borrowers with a heightened risk of default, such as those with a history of loan delinquency or default, bankruptcy, limited debt experience, uncertain future income prospects, etc. These became very popular in some regions of the United States where sub-prime mortgages were offered to unemployed buyers and illegal immigrants. The issuer of the sub-prime instruments bundled the mortgages with other loans and sold them as short-term investments through banks and brokerages for distribution to other investors. (See ASSET-BACKED COMMERCIAL PAPER [ABCP], page 128.)

ABOUT THE AUTHOR

Bestselling author JOHN LAWRENCE REYNOLDS has written extensively on business, finance and investment matters. His book *Free Rider* won the National Business Book Award, and *The Naked Investor* hit national top financial book lists twice, with two editions. He is also the author of books on leading Canadian politicians and business people, including Air Canada CEO Robert Milton (*Straight from the Top*), former federal minister and Newfoundland premier Brian Tobin (*All in Good Time*), legendary entrepreneur Craig Dobbin (*One Hell of a Ride*) and Buzz Hargrove of the Canadian Auto Workers (a biography soon to be released).